FUN

Tinkle, Tinkle little car
How I wonder what you are.

Leaking oil every day
Having it your own way.

Going up hills real slow
I don't want you any mo'.

Tinkle, Tinkle little car
Boy, what a lemon you are.

....

Well, my daddy left home when I was three,
and he didn't leave much to Ma and me,
just this old guitar and a bottle of booze.
Now I don't blame him because he run and hid,
but the meanest thing that he ever did was
before he left he went and named me Sue.

Well, he must have thought it was quite a joke,
and it got lots of laughs from a lot of folks,
it seems I had to fight my whole life through.
Some gal would giggle and I'd get red
and some guy would laugh and I'd bust his head,
I tell you, life ain't easy for a boy named Sue.

Well, I grew up quick and I grew up mean.

FUNNY POEMS

My fist got hard and my wits got keen.
Roamed from town to town to hide my shame,
but I made me a vow to the moon and the stars,
I'd search the honky tonks and bars and kill
that man that gave me that awful name.

But it was Gatlinburg in mid July and I had
just hit town and my throat was dry.
I'd thought i'd stop and have myself a brew.
At an old saloon in a street of mud
and at a table dealing stud sat the dirty,
mangy dog that named me Sue.

Well, I knew that snake was my own sweet dad
from a worn-out picture that my mother had
and I knew the scar on his cheek and his evil eye.
He was big and bent and gray and old
and I looked at him and my blood ran cold,
and I said, "My name is Sue. How do you do?
Now you're gonna die." Yeah, that's what I told
him.

Well, I hit him right between the eyes and he went
down
but to my surprise he came up with a knife
and cut off a piece of my ear. But I busted a chair
right across his teeth. And we crashed through
the wall and into the street kicking and a-gouging
in the mud and the blood and the beer.

FUNNY POEMS

I tell you I've fought tougher men but I really can't
remember when.
He kicked like a mule and bit like a crocodile.
I heard him laughin' and then I heard him cussin',
he went for his gun and I pulled mine first.
He stood there looking at me and I saw him smile.

And he said, "Son, this world is rough and if
a man's gonna make it, he's gotta be tough
and I knew I wouldn't be there to help you along.
So I gave you that name and I said 'Goodbye'.
I knew you'd have to get tough or die. And it's
that name that helped to make you strong."

Yeah, he said, "Now you have just fought one
helluva fight, and I know you hate me and you've
got the right to kill me now and I wouldn't blame
you
if you do. But you ought to thank me
before I die for the gravel in your guts and the spit
in your eye because I'm the guy that named you
Sue."
Yeah, what could I do? What could I do?

I got all choked up and I threw down my gun,
called him pa and he called me a son,
and I came away with a different point of view
and I think about him now and then.
Every time I tried, every time I win and if I
ever have a son I think I am gonna name him
Bill or George - anything but Sue.

FUNNY POEMS

....

My son gifted me a phone, said it was very smart.
He said it would ease my life, that it was a new start.

Connect to internet, search for all you want to know.
No need for TV; on it, watch your favorite show.

It's time to throw out your ancient alarm clock.
You can shop for anything, from a ship to a sock.

You can find every address with the hi-tech map.
You can get rid of the wrinkles on your photo with an app.

You can pay your bills online with a single click.
You can order a meal, with just a finger-flick.

Now you can chat and tweet from your armchair.
Photos of your grandkids you can see and share.

You have the world at your fingertips now, said he,
But I struggle to make a simple call, Stupid Old Me!

I wanted to send a message to my oldest friend.
For dear, I typed dead and then pressed send.

FUNNY POEMS

I tried to watch a movie, but it made my eyes spin.
How to see those mini-figures on a tiny screen.

I tried to use the calculator; it took me an hour to
find.
I could have added up the numbers faster in my
mind.

Things get opened and switched on without my
will.
I break into a sweat at the thought of my data bill.

Stop sending me "Good day texts" for goodness
sake.
Those pings and rings give me a blasting
headache.

So, for others, a smart phone may be trendy and
hot.
For me, it's useless; as it's smart, but I am not.

....

I've fallen in love- I don't know why
I've fallen in love with a girl with one eye.

I knew from the start. It was plain to see
That this wonderful girl had an eye out for me

She's charming and witty and jolly and jocular

FUNNY POEMS

Not what you'd expect from a girl who's
monocular.

Of eyes - at the moment - she hasn't full quota
But that doesn't change things for me one iota.

It must be quite difficult if you're bereft.
If your left eye is gone and your right eye is left.

But she's made up her mind. She's made her
decision.
She can see it quite clearly in 10/20 vision.

She'll not leave me waiting, not left in the lurch
If she looks slightly sideways she'll see me in
church.

I'll marry my true love who's gentle and kind.
And thus prove to everyone that loves not quite
blind.

....

I need to lose weight, just a pound or twenty.
If I could lose fifty, well that would be plenty.
I could join a gym, but I don't have the gumption.
My legging clad legs aren't for public
consumption.

My exercise bike is succumbing to rust

And only gets touched when I really must dust.
And much like a pet in need of attention,
It made me feel guilty (and slack not to mention).

The solution, of course, was such a no brainer.
I bought it a mate...an elliptical trainer!
This is quite easy! Or so I reckoned
When I tried it in store for a whole fifteen seconds.

But once it was home and I tried it for longer,
The pain in my side was all that got stronger.
I puffed and I gasped, till I couldn't breathe.
Kicked off at nine, it was now nine oh three.

Of course! The resistance must be way too high
But no, it read zero; I thought I might cry.
The six on the dial sat silently mocking,
My level of fitness was really quite shocking.

Motivation was all that I saw myself losing,
And my self-esteem was taking a bruising.
I tried it to music but all that achieved
It drowned out the sound of my poor creaking
knees.

This instrument of torture could go take a hike.
I glanced now with longing at my trusty bike.
I couldn't recall why we had parted ways.
Climbed up on the seat and thought, Happy days!

I pedalled with gusto, but soon I remembered...

FUNNY POEMS

It felt like my buttocks were being dismembered.
The padding on my derrière is quite thick,
So why does it feel like I'm perched on a brick?

It was just all too hard; I gave up in disgust.
My plan to lose weight was clearly a bust.
Oh well...at least I can say that I tried it.
I mean, really, I can't be expected to diet!

....

Restful sleep has proved elusive.
Lack of it is not conducive
To my overall wellbeing,
As I stare up at the ceiling.

Niggling aches and pains compound
To stop my sleep from being sound.
I toss and turn from side to side,
But all positions have been tried.

I am by all accounts quite round,
But when it comes to sleep, I've found
I wish I were more octagon -
A full eight sides to rotate on.

To lie flat on my back does tempt,
Though soon I find I must pre-empt
The snores I'm told will wake the dead
By rolling on my side instead.

And finally, I find my groove,
Then curse because I have to move.
The electric blanket's getting hot
And on this side the switch is not.

If comfyness arrives too late,
I'll feel the urge to urinate.
And once that tickle is perceived,
It soon demands to be relieved.

I do my utmost to ignore,
But know I'll have to go before
This little twinge of urgency
Becomes full blown emergency.

I hit the loo and park it there
With just a nanosec to spare.
Sit a while and contemplate
How so much could accumulate!

Back in bed, it starts again,
The quest to find my inner zen.
Must stop my thoughts from swirling round,
The ideal pozzy must be found.

At last my eyelids start to droop.
Don't need to pee, don't need to poop.
But then with dread I feel the heat
Rising upwards from my feet.

A damned hot flush is taking hold

And now I'm longing for the cold!
Sheet and quilt are tossed aside,
Must suffer through till it subsides.

Once again, I know I've failed.
Won't wake bright-eyed and bushy-tailed.
I'll have no pep, I'll have no zing.
Rise and shine is not my thing.

I can't believe it's come to this.
I've tried my hardest to resist.
In order to not feel like crap,
I must embrace the nanna nap!

....

They put me in the oven to bake.
Me, a deprived and miserable cake.
Feeling the heat, I started to bubble.
Watching the others, I knew I was in trouble.

They opened the door and I started my life.
Frosting me with a silver knife,
Decorating me with candy jewels.
The rest of my batch looked like fools.

Lifting me up, she took off my wrapper.
Feeling the breeze, I wanted to slap her.
Opening her mouth with shiny teeth inside,

FUNNY POEMS

This was the day this cupcake died.

....

'Twas the eve before Christmas.
I left it too late.
The shelves are all bare.
Oh, why did I wait?

I swore I'd shop early,
I clearly remember,
And be done with it all
By the first of December.

But now here I am
With picked-over stock.
The boxes are crumpled
On the Marvel knockoffs.

Sweaters too big,
Slippers too small.
The pushing the grabbing,
Get me out of this mall.

I will stop at the drug store
And purchase a card
And fill it with money.
Why make life hard?

It always fits
And suits everyone's taste.

No need to wrap it.
That's just a waste.

But should you not like it,
Dear, have no fear,
If you'd like to return it,
My pocket's right here.

....

Pretty little high heels,
How you look so grand.
I can remember when I wore you
And I could proudly stand.

Now you look kind of scary,
Sitting on my closet shelf.
I want to put you on,
But I don't trust myself.

Just a few short years ago,
I could wear you and actual walk.
But now that's just a memory
Of which I happily talk.

Oh, my little high heels,
I did not have a clue
That one day you would frighten me
And I would stay away from you.

FUNNY POEMS

I'm seeing that my golden years
Are robbing me of things like you.
Now I shop in the senior section,
Something I thought I'd never do.

It's not that I don't love you,
But I'm up against a wall,
For to wear you once again
Would mean a nasty fall.

I still dream of wearing you,
But to flats I am bound,
For they're the only shoes I trust
To keep me firmly on the ground.

....

"I cannot go to school today,"
Said little Peggy Ann McKay.
"I have the measles and the mumps,
A gash, a rash and purple bumps.
My mouth is wet, my throat is dry,
I'm going blind in my right eye.
My tonsils are as big as rocks,
I've counted sixteen chicken pox
And there's one more--that's seventeen,
And don't you think my face looks green?
My leg is cut--my eyes are blue--
It might be instamatic flu.
I cough and sneeze and gasp and choke,

FUNNY POEMS

I’m sure that my left leg is broke--
My hip hurts when I move my chin,
My belly button’s caving in,
My back is wrenched, my ankle’s sprained,
My ‘pendix pains each time it rains.
My nose is cold, my toes are numb.
I have a sliver in my thumb.
My neck is stiff, my voice is weak,
I hardly whisper when I speak.
My tongue is filling up my mouth,
I think my hair is falling out.
My elbow’s bent, my spine ain’t straight,
My temperature is one-o-eight.
My brain is shrunk, I cannot hear,
There is a hole inside my ear.
I have a hangnail, and my heart is--what?
What’s that? What’s that you say?
You say today is. . .Saturday?
G’bye, I’m going out to play!”

....

The other night 'bout two o'clock, or maybe it was three,
An elephant with shining tusks came chasing after me.
His trunk was wavin' in the air an' spoutin' jets of steam
An' he was out to eat me up, but still I didn't scream

Or let him see that I was scared - a better thought I had,
I just escaped from where I was and crawled in bed with Dad.

One time there was a giant who was horrible to see,
He had three heads and twenty arms, an' he came after me
And red hot fire came from his mouths and every hand was red
And he declared he'd grind my bones and make them into bread.
But I was just too smart for him, I fooled him mighty bad,
Before his hands could collar me I crawled in bed with Dad.

I ain't scared of nothin' that comes pesterin' me at night.
Once I was chased by forty ghosts all shimmery an' white.
An' I just raced 'em round the room an' let 'em think maybe
I'd have to stop an' rest awhile, when they could capture me.
Then when they leapt onto my bed, Oh Gee! But they were mad
To find that I had slipped away an' crawled in bed with Dad.

FUNNY POEMS

No giants, ghosts or elephants have dared to come in there
'Coz if they did he'd beat 'em up and chase 'em to their lair.
They just hang 'round the children's rooms
an' snap an' snarl an' bite
An' laugh if they can make 'em yell
for help with all their might.
But I don't ever yell out loud. I'm not that sort of lad,
I slip from out the covers and I crawl in bed with Dad.

....

I made myself a snowball
As perfect as could be.
I thought I'd keep it as a pet
And let it sleep with me.
I made it some pajamas
And a pillow for its head.
Then last night it ran away,
But first it wet the bed.

....

I own a big fat cat-
The fattest for miles around.
Wherever there's lots of food,

That's where he'll be found.

He's really good at eating.
It's a talent, I suppose.
I'm sure if he keeps at it
He'd win the talent shows.

I own a big fat cat-
He weighs at least a ton.
He couldn't run to save his life.
Yes, he isn't much fun.

His favourite room's the kitchen.
(I'm sure we all know why.)
He eats just about everything,
So that's why, with a sigh...

I'd like to tell you, Teacher,
I'd like to tell you straight,
I might have "accidentally" dropped
My homework in his plate.

....

When I got home from camp today,
My parents almost died.
They asked me how I got this way,
And here's what I replied:

This little cast from heel to hip
Is nothing much at all.

FUNNY POEMS

Some broken shingles made me slip
From off the dining hall.

The poison ivy's not too bad.
It missed my back and chest.
Of course, I guess I oughta add
Mosquitoes got the rest.

I tried to eat some hick'ry nuts
And cracked a tooth or two.
And all these bruises, scabs, and cuts?
I haven't got a clue.

I got the lump that's on my head
From diving in the lake.
I should've watched for rocks instead
Of grabbing for the snake.

That leaves this bandage on my chin
And these three finger sprains,
Along with lots of sunburned skin
And sniffles from the rains.

I also got a muscle cramp
And very nearly drowned.
It's some terrific summer camp,
The coolest one around.

....

FUNNY POEMS

Hear eye sit inn English class; the likelihood is that eye won't pass
An F on my report card wood bee worse than swallowing glass
It's knot that eye haven't studied, often till late at knight
Butt the rules are sew confusing, eye simply can't get them write

Hour teacher says, "Heed my advice, ewe must study and sacrifice"
Butt if mouses are mice and louses are lice, how come blouses aren't blice
The confusion really abounds when adding esses two nouns
Gooses are geese, butt mooses aren't meese; somebody scent in the clowns

Two ultimatums are ultimata, and a couple of datum are data
Sew wouldn't ewe expect it wood bee correct fore a bunch of plums to be plata?
And if more than won octopus are octopi, and the plural of ox is oxen
Shouldn't a couple of busses bee bussi and a pare of foxes bee foxen?

Let's talk about spelling a wile, specifically letters witch are silent
Words like "psychologist" and "wreck" shirley make awl of us violent

FUNNY POEMS

And another example quite plane witch is really hard two explain
If it's eye before e except after sea, then what about feign and reign?

The final exam will determine how eye due, weather eye pass ore fail
I halve prepared as much as eye can down two the last detail
I'm ready two give it my vary best inn just a little wile
And then isle take a relaxing wrest on a tropical aisle

....

The day when the world
turned upside down:
when a frown became a smile
and a smile became a frown.

When the mice chased the cats
the cats chased the dogs.
The dogs laughed out loud
at the pink and yellow frogs.

When you went to bed in the daytime
and got up at night.
When birds caught the school bus
and the cows took flight.

FUNNY POEMS

When the moon came out
in the middle of the day
and all of the ocean's fish
rolled around in the hay.

When the children ruled the world
and ice cream was for free
and the elephants shrank
to the size of a flea.

When the grass rained lollipops
up to the sky.
When you wanted to laugh
but could only cry.

When magic beans were real
and giants very small,
you would eat spiders legs
so you could creep up the wall.

This all happened when the
world turned upside down
after I went to bed
with a smile - not a frown.

....

Christopher Robin
Had wheezles
And sneezles,

FUNNY POEMS

They bundled him
Into
His bed.
They gave him what goes
With a cold in the nose,
And some more for a cold
In the head.
They wondered
If wheezles
Could turn
Into measles,
If sneezles
Would turn
Into mumps;
They examined his chest
For a rash,
And the rest
Of his body for swellings and lumps.
They sent for some doctors
In sneezles
And wheezles
To tell them what ought
To be done.
All sorts and conditions
Of famous physicians
Came hurrying round
At a run.
They all made a note
Of the state of his throat,
They asked if he suffered from thirst;
They asked if the sneezles

Came after the wheezles,
Or if the first sneezle
Came first.
They said, "If you teazle
A sneezle
Or wheezle,
A measle
May easily grow.
But humour or pleazle
The wheezle
Or sneezle,
The measle
Will certainly go."
They expounded the reazles
For sneezles
And wheezles,
The manner of measles
When new.
They said "If he freezles
In draughts and in breezles,
Then PHTHEEZLES
May even ensue."

Christopher Robin
Got up in the morning,
The sneezles had vanished away.
And the look in his eye
Seemed to say to the sky,
"Now, how to amuse them to-day?"
....

FUNNY POEMS

Whosever room this is should be ashamed!
His underwear is hanging on the lamp.
His raincoat is there in the overstuffed chair,
And the chair is becoming quite mucky and damp.
His workbook is wedged in the window,
His sweater's been thrown on the floor.
His scarf and one ski are beneath the TV,
And his pants have been carelessly hung on the
door.
His books are all jammed in the closet,
His vest has been left in the hall.
A lizard named Ed is asleep in his bed,
And his smelly old sock has been stuck to the wall.
Whosever room this is should be ashamed!
Donald or Robert or Willie or--
Huh? You say it's mine? Oh, dear,
I knew it looked familiar!

....

Halfway down the stairs
Is a stair
Where I sit.
There isn't any
Other stair
Quite like
It.
I'm not at the bottom,
I'm not at the top;

FUNNY POEMS

So this is the stair
Where
I always
Stop.

Halfway up the stairs
Isn't up
And isn't down.
It isn't in the nursery,
It isn't in the town.
And all sorts of funny thoughts
Run round my head.
It isn't really
Anywhere!
It's somewhere else
Instead!

....

I've hunted near, I've hunted far
I even looked inside my car.
I've lost my glasses, I'm in need,
To have them now so I can read.
I loudly swear and I curse
Did I leave them in my purse?
Are they behind the sofa, under the bed?
Oh there they are - on my head!

....

FUNNY POEMS

All doggies go to heaven (or so I've been told).
They run and play along the streets of gold.
Why is heaven such a doggie-delight?
Why, because there's not a single cat in sight!

,,,,,,,,,,,,,,,,,,,,,,

When I'm old and mankey,
I'll never use a hanky.
I'll wee on plants
and soil my pants
and sometimes get quite cranky.

....

I once knew a man who lived in a jar.
For a stranger sight you'd have to go far.
I asked him once why he lived in a jar.
He grimaced and said, how bizarre you are.

My jar's so cozy, warm and bright,
Even in the full moonlight.
The only drawback is, you see,
Getting out quickly when I have to pee.

....

I didn't go to church today,
I trust the Lord to understand.
The surf was swirling blue and white,
The children swirling on the sand.

FUNNY POEMS

He knows, He knows how brief my stay,
How brief this spell of summer weather,
He knows when I am said and done
We'll have plenty of time together

....

I guess you think you know this story.
You don't. The real one's much more gory.
The phoney one, the one you know,
Was cooked up years and years ago,
And made to sound all soft and sappy
just to keep the children happy.
Mind you, they got the first bit right,
The bit where, in the dead of night,
The Ugly Sisters, jewels and all,
Departed for the Palace Ball,
While darling little Cinderella
Was locked up in a slimy cellar,
Where rats who wanted things to eat,
Began to nibble at her feet.

She bellowed 'Help!' and 'Let me out!
The Magic Fairy heard her shout.
Appearing in a blaze of light,
She said: 'My dear, are you all right?'
'All right?' cried Cindy .'Can't you see
'I feel as rotten as can be!'
She beat her fist against the wall,
And shouted, 'Get me to the Ball!
'There is a Disco at the Palace!

'The rest have gone and I am jealous!
'I want a dress! I want a coach!
'And earrings and a diamond brooch!
'And silver slippers, two of those!
'And lovely nylon panty hose!
'Done up like that I'll guarantee
'The handsome Prince will fall for me!'
The Fairy said, 'Hang on a tick.'
She gave her wand a mighty flick
And quickly, in no time at all,
Cindy was at the Palace Ball!

It made the Ugly Sisters wince
To see her dancing with the Prince.
She held him very tight and pressed
herself against his manly chest.
The Prince himself was turned to pulp,
All he could do was gasp and gulp.
Then midnight struck. She shouted, 'Heck!
I've got to run to save my neck!'
The Prince cried, 'No! Alas! Alack!'
He grabbed her dress to hold her back.
As Cindy shouted, 'Let me go!'
The dress was ripped from head to toe.

She ran out in her underwear,
And lost one slipper on the stair.
The Prince was on it like a dart,
He pressed it to his pounding heart,
'The girl this slipper fits,' he cried,
'Tomorrow morn shall be my bride!

I'll visit every house in town
'Until I've tracked the maiden down!'
Then rather carelessly, I fear,
He placed it on a crate of beer.

At once, one of the Ugly Sisters,
(The one whose face was blotched with blisters)
Sneaked up and grabbed the dainty shoe,
And quickly flushed it down the loo.
Then in its place she calmly put
The slipper from her own left foot.
Ah ha, you see, the plot grows thicker,
And Cindy's luck starts looking sicker.

Next day, the Prince went charging down
To knock on all the doors in town.
In every house, the tension grew.
Who was the owner of the shoe?
The shoe was long and very wide.
(A normal foot got lost inside.)
Also it smelled a wee bit icky.
(The owner's feet were hot and sticky.)
Thousands of eager people came
To try it on, but all in vain.
Now came the Ugly Sisters' go.
One tried it on. The Prince screamed, 'No!'
But she screamed, 'Yes! It fits! Whoopee!
'So now you've got to marry me!'
The Prince went white from ear to ear.
He muttered, 'Let me out of here.'
'Oh no you don't! You made a vow!

'There's no way you can back out now!'
'Off with her head!' The Prince roared back.
They chopped it off with one big whack.
This pleased the Prince. He smiled and said,
'She's prettier without her head.'
Then up came Sister Number Two,
Who yelled, 'Now I will try the shoe!'
'Try this instead!' the Prince yelled back.
He swung his trusty sword and smack
Her head went crashing to the ground.
It bounced a bit and rolled around.
In the kitchen, peeling spuds,
Cinderella heard the thuds
Of bouncing heads upon the floor,
And poked her own head round the door.
'What's all the racket? 'Cindy cried.
'Mind your own bizz,' the Prince replied.
Poor Cindy's heart was torn to shreds.
My Prince! she thought. He chops off heads!
How could I marry anyone
Who does that sort of thing for fun?

The Prince cried, 'Who's this dirty slut?
'Off with her nut! Off with her nut!'
Just then, all in a blaze of light,
The Magic Fairy hove in sight,
Her Magic Wand went swoosh and swish!
'Cindy! 'she cried, 'come make a wish!
'Wish anything and have no doubt
'That I will make it come about!'
Cindy answered, 'Oh kind Fairy,

FUNNY POEMS

'This time I shall be more wary.
'No more Princes, no more money.
'I have had my taste of honey.
I'm wishing for a decent man.
'They're hard to find. D'you think you can?'
Within a minute, Cinderella
Was married to a lovely feller,
A simple jam maker by trade,
Who sold good home-made marmalade.
Their house was filled with smiles and laughter
And they were happy ever after.

....

The animal I really dig,
Above all others is the pig.
Pigs are noble. Pigs are clever,
Pigs are courteous. However,
Now and then, to break this rule,
One meets a pig who is a fool.
What, for example, would you say,
If strolling through the woods one day,
Right there in front of you you saw
A pig who'd built his house of STRAW?
The Wolf who saw it licked his lips,
And said, 'That pig has had his chips.'
'Little pig, little pig, let me come in!'
'No, no, by the hairs on my chinny-chin-chin!'
'Then I'll huff and I'll puff and I'll blow your house in!'

The little pig began to pray,
But Wolfie blew his house away.
He shouted, 'Bacon, pork and ham!
Oh, what a lucky Wolf I am!'
And though he ate the pig quite fast,
He carefully kept the tail till last.
Wolf wandered on, a trifle bloated.
Surprise, surprise, for soon he noted
Another little house for pigs,
And this one had been built of TWIGS!

'Little pig, little pig, let me come in!'
'No, no, by the hairs on my chinny-chin-chin!'
'Then I'll huff and I'll puff and I'll blow your house in!'

The Wolf said, 'Okay, here we go!'
He then began to blow and blow.
The little pig began to squeal.
He cried, 'Oh Wolf, you've had one meal!
Why can't we talk and make a deal?
The Wolf replied, 'Not on your nelly!'
And soon the pig was in his belly.

'Two juicy little pigs!' Wolf cried,
'But still I'm not quite satisfied!
I know how full my tummy's bulging,
But oh, how I adore indulging.'
So creeping quietly as a mouse,
The Wolf approached another house,
A house which also had inside

FUNNY POEMS

A little piggy trying to hide.
'You'll not get me!' the Piggy cried.
'I'll blow you down!' the Wolf replied.
'You'll need,' Pig said, 'a lot of puff,
And I don't think you've got enough.'
Wolf huffed and puffed and blew and blew.
The house stayed up as good as new.
'If I can't blow it down,' Wolf said,
I'll have to blow it up instead.
I'll come back in the dead of night
And blow it up with dynamite!'
Pig cried, 'You brute! I might have known!'
Then, picking up the telephone,
He dialed as quickly as he could
The number of red Riding Hood.

'Hello,' she said. 'Who's speaking? Who?
Oh, hello, Piggy, how d'you do?'
Pig cried, 'I need your help, Miss Hood!
Oh help me, please! D'you think you could?'
'I'll try of course,' Miss Hood replied.
'What's on your mind...?' 'A Wolf!' Pig cried.
'I know you've dealt with wolves before,
And now I've got one at my door!'

'My darling Pig,' she said, 'my sweet,
That's something really up my street.
I've just begun to wash my hair.
But when it's dry, I'll be right there.'

A short while later, through the wood,

Came striding brave Miss Riding Hood.
The Wolf stood there, his eyes ablaze,
And yellowish, like mayonnaise.
His teeth were sharp, his gums were raw,
And spit was dripping from his jaw.
Once more the maiden's eyelid flickers.
She draws the pistol from her knickers.
Once more she hits the vital spot,
And kills him with a single shot.
Pig, peeping through the window, stood
And yelled, 'Well done, Miss Riding Hood!'

Ah, Piglet, you must never trust
Young ladies from the upper crust.
For now, Miss Riding Hood, one notes,
Not only has two wolfskin coats,
But when she goes from place to place,
She has a PIGSKIN TRAVELING CASE.

....

In England once there lived a big
And wonderfully clever pig.
To everybody it was plain
That Piggy had a massive brain.
He worked out sums inside his head,
There was no book he hadn't read.
He knew what made an airplane fly,
He knew how engines worked and why.
He knew all this, but in the end
One question drove him round the bend:

FUNNY POEMS

He simply couldn't puzzle out
What LIFE was really all about.
What was the reason for his birth?
Why was he placed upon this earth?
His giant brain went round and round.
Alas, no answer could be found.
Till suddenly one wondrous night.
All in a flash he saw the light.
He jumped up like a ballet dancer
And yelled, 'By gum, I've got the answer! '
'They want my bacon slice by slice
'To sell at a tremendous price!
'They want my tender juicy chops
'To put in all the butcher's shops!
'They want my pork to make a roast
'And that's the part'll cost the most!
'They want my sausages in strings!
'They even want my chitterlings!
'The butcher's shop! The carving knife!
'That is the reason for my life! '
Such thoughts as these are not designed
To give a pig great peace of mind.
Next morning, in comes Farmer Bland,
A pail of pigswill in his hand,
And piggy with a mighty roar,
Bashes the farmer to the floor…
Now comes the rather grisly bit
So let's not make too much of it,
Except that you must understand
That Piggy did eat Farmer Bland,
He ate him up from head to toe,

Chewing the pieces nice and slow.
It took an hour to reach the feet,
Because there was so much to eat,
And when he finished, Pig, of course,
Felt absolutely no remorse.
Slowly he scratched his brainy head
And with a little smile he said,
'I had a fairly powerful hunch
'That he might have me for his lunch.
'And so, because I feared the worst,
'I thought I'd better eat him first.'

....

As soon as Wolf began to feel
That he would like a decent meal,
He went and knocked on Grandma's door.
When Grandma opened it, she saw
The sharp white teeth, the horrid grin,
And Wolfie said, 'May I come in?'
Poor Grandmamma was terrified,
'He's going to eat me up!' she cried.
And she was absolutely right.
He ate her up in one big bite.
But Grandmamma was small and tough,
And Wolfie wailed, 'That's not enough!
I haven't yet begun to feel
That I have had a decent meal!'
He ran around the kitchen yelping,
'I've got to have a second helping!'

Then added with a frightful leer,
'I'm therefore going to wait right here
Till Little Miss Red Riding Hood
Comes home from walking in the wood.'

He quickly put on Grandma's clothes,
(Of course he hadn't eaten those).
He dressed himself in coat and hat.
He put on shoes, and after that,
He even brushed and curled his hair,
Then sat himself in Grandma's chair.

In came the little girl in red.
She stopped. She stared. And then she said,
'What great big ears you have, Grandma.'
'All the better to hear you with,'
the Wolf replied.
'What great big eyes you have, Grandma.'
said Little Red Riding Hood.
'All the better to see you with,'
the Wolf replied.
He sat there watching her and smiled.
He thought, I'm going to eat this child.
Compared with her old Grandmamma,
She's going to taste like caviar.

Then Little Red Riding Hood said, '
But Grandma, what a lovely great big
furry coat you have on.'

'That's wrong!' cried Wolf.

FUNNY POEMS

'Have you forgot
To tell me what BIG TEETH I've got?
Ah well, no matter what you say,
I'm going to eat you anyway.'

The small girl smiles. One eyelid flickers.
She whips a pistol from her knickers.
She aims it at the creature's head,
And bang bang bang, she shoots him dead.

A few weeks later, in the wood,
I came across Miss Riding Hood.
But what a change! No cloak of red,
No silly hood upon her head.
She said, 'Hello, and do please note
My lovely furry wolfskin coat.'

....

My new phone is "smart." I guess that I'm not.
Amazing what all this here smart phone has got.
TV and Weather and Internet, too.
There's just no limits to what it can do.
Check my blood pressure and my temperature
Without even probing all my apertures.
I now know the time in Paris or Greece.
I can track the migration of thousands of geese
Or find Chinese food; it's here on this map.
Oops, my finger just slipped, now where was that at?
A camera...a CAMERA! Now I can take shots

FUNNY POEMS

Of everyone I know (who'd rather I not).
Push this here button and take me a "selfie."
(If it had a nose would this thing take a
"smellfie"?)
Email to pester with, video to shoot,
Maps to drive 'round with, wow that's a hoot!
A compass to guide me home if I'm lost.
Thank God work paid for this thing (what it
COSTS!).
The things that it does would amaze Mr. Bell.
What he would have thought of it, no one can tell,
But one question's still stuck in my middle-aged
craw.
Despite all the gizmos that strike me with awe,
They're fun and they're useful and "techy" and all
...But how do I just simply make a phone call?

....

Well, the dishes are done,
There's nothing in the sink.
So I think I'll sit,
And pour myself a drink.
But just as I sit,
I hear her voice.
And I've got to get up,
Because I've got no choice.

You see, I've got this woman,
Who says she's my wife.

And says I promised to love her,
For the rest of my life.
She's awful bossy,
And overbearing too.
And she loves to tell me,
What to do!

She says, "Ronald, are the dishes done?
Did you wash and dry each one?
Ronald, did you put them away,
Don't you listen to what I say?"

And I say,

"Yes, Dear, the dishes are done,
I washed and dried each one.
Yes, Dear, I put them away,
Because I always do whatever you say."

But I don't know why,
I let her treat me this way.
And I swear to God,
I'm going to leave her some day.
I'm going to walk out,
And I'm going to have some fun.
But until that day,
The dishes will be done.

....

Big, fat Santa bounded through my halls;

FUNNY POEMS

He made everything shake, even the walls.

He ate all my cookies,
Drank all my milk;

He had heavy boots,
And a coat made of silk.

Over his back he carried the toys;
Some of them, a lot of them, even made noise.

He smelled like fresh, tobacco smoke;
He gave my favorite tree an irritated poke.

A grumpy look came upon his face;
This guy is crazy, and I bet he carries mace.

He reached into his bag, so I thought for gold,
But out he pulled, a big lump of coal.

With an angry look, he set it down with ease;
Then walked up to my chimney, and gave his nose
a squeeze.

I'll never forget the obese man in red;
I'll hate him forever, until the day I am dead.

....

FUNNY POEMS

Many, many years ago
When I was just a kid,
And I had just began to grow,
There's stuff I had and did.

I'm thinking back on all those things
That life saw fit to give me.
If I can't remember everything,
I hope you will forgive me.

Chocolate candy cigarettes
And big bubble gum cigars.
Mini Bricks and Red Ball Jets,
Hopscotch and Dinky cars.

Mercurochrome and iodine;
Band-aids in a can.
Your watch required a daily wind,
And Etch-A-Sketch was grand.

In school, the teacher had to see
Just what you had to do.
You held one finger up for pee;
You held up two for poo!

Marbles, Slinkys, Lincoln Logs,
Ker Plunk and Pick Up Sticks,
With Yo-yos, you could "walk the dog,"

FUNNY POEMS

And ice cream came in bricks.

Arrows all had suction cups
And guns had rolls of caps.
Paddle Balls and Tonka Trucks
Big red lips were wax,

Bumps on heads, being black and blue,
Was minor when compared to
Being sick with cold or flu!
Have fun? You're not prepared to!

Measles, mumps, and chicken pox
Always seemed to flare.
They opened up Pandora's Box
And caught us unaware!

With medicine and care from mom,
Our time in bed was cut!
But I can't remember anyone
Allergic to a nut!

Nancy Drew and Hardy Boys
And also Brothers Grimm.
But Mark Twain was my pride and joy!
I never could resist him!

Hide and seek and tag were there.

New energy we found!
No more teacher scorns to bear
When summer came around.

PF Flyer running shoes,
Steel roller skates had keys.
There were phone booths we could use
If there's emergencies.

Rolling down a grassy hill
In parks was a delight.
Nicky Nine Doors was a thrill,
But only played at night!

We rode our bikes with playing cards
Flapping on our spokes.
We played in all our friends' backyards
And told our "Knock Knock" jokes.

Climbing fences, climbing trees
Were common things to do.
Getting bruised or skinning knees?
That was nothing new!

Two wheel scooters, kiddy cars,
We had Soap Box Rallies.
Baseball teams and monkey bars
And close by bowling alleys.

FUNNY POEMS

In winter, there were snowball fights
And snow forts for protection.
And when a bitter wind would bite,
Few kids raised objection!

Speeding down a snowy slope
On sleds and blown up tires.
"Is it too steep?" We all said, "Nope!"
We wanted to go higher!

In our teens were Levi jeans,
Duck and pony tails.
Sock hops were a common scene
Where dancing would prevail.

Bobby socks and poodle skirts
And continental slacks.
White buck shoes and fancy shirts,
Guitars and wailing sax!

Computers? What on Earth were they?!
Well, they would show up later.
And none I knew could dare display
Cell phones or calculators!

Many things I've mentioned here
Are still with us today.

But lots of kids, it does appear,
Ignore this great buffet!

What happened to the world I knew?
Have kids today stopped growing?
If time machines were really true,
I know where I'd be going!

Dick, Jane, Spot and Puff
Are nothing now but jokes.
But maybe I have said enough,
So I'll say, "That's all folks!"

....

The most important thing we've learned,
So far as children are concerned,
Is never, NEVER, NEVER let
Them near your television set --
Or better still, just don't install
The idiotic thing at all.
In almost every house we've been,
We've watched them gaping at the screen.
They loll and slop and lounge about,
And stare until their eyes pop out.
(Last week in someone's place we saw
A dozen eyeballs on the floor.)
They sit and stare and stare and sit

Until they're hypnotised by it,
Until they're absolutely drunk
With all that shocking ghastly junk.
Oh yes, we know it keeps them still,
They don't climb out the window sill,
They never fight or kick or punch,
They leave you free to cook the lunch
And wash the dishes in the sink --
But did you ever stop to think,
To wonder just exactly what
This does to your beloved tot?
IT ROTS THE SENSE IN THE HEAD!
IT KILLS IMAGINATION DEAD!
IT CLOGS AND CLUTTERS UP THE MIND!
IT MAKES A CHILD SO DULL AND BLIND
HE CAN NO LONGER UNDERSTAND
A FANTASY, A FAIRYLAND!
HIS BRAIN BECOMES AS SOFT AS CHEESE!
HIS POWERS OF THINKING RUST AND FREEZE!
HE CANNOT THINK -- HE ONLY SEES!
'All right!' you'll cry. 'All right!' you'll say,
'But if we take the set away,
What shall we do to entertain
Our darling children? Please explain!'
We'll answer this by asking you,
'What used the darling ones to do?
'How used they keep themselves contented
Before this monster was invented?'

FUNNY POEMS

Have you forgotten? Don't you know?
We'll say it very loud and slow:
THEY ... USED ... TO ... READ! They'd READ and
READ,
AND READ and READ, and then proceed
To READ some more. Great Scott! Gadzooks!
One half their lives was reading books!
The nursery shelves held books galore!
Books cluttered up the nursery floor!
And in the bedroom, by the bed,
More books were waiting to be read!
Such wondrous, fine, fantastic tales
Of dragons, gypsies, queens, and whales
And treasure isles, and distant shores
Where smugglers rowed with muffled oars,
And pirates wearing purple pants,
And sailing ships and elephants,
And cannibals crouching 'round the pot,
Stirring away at something hot.
(It smells so good, what can it be?
Good gracious, it's Penelope.)
The younger ones had Beatrix Potter
With Mr. Tod, the dirty rotter,
And Squirrel Nutkin, Pigling Bland,
And Mrs. Tiggy-Winkle and-
Just How The Camel Got His Hump,
And How the Monkey Lost His Rump,
And Mr. Toad, and bless my soul,

FUNNY POEMS

There's Mr. Rat and Mr. Mole-
Oh, books, what books they used to know,
Those children living long ago!
So please, oh please, we beg, we pray,
Go throw your TV set away,
And in its place you can install
A lovely bookshelf on the wall.
Then fill the shelves with lots of books,
Ignoring all the dirty looks,
The screams and yells, the bites and kicks,
And children hitting you with sticks-
Fear not, because we promise you
That, in about a week or two
Of having nothing else to do,
They'll now begin to feel the need
Of having something to read.
And once they start -- oh boy, oh boy!
You watch the slowly growing joy
That fills their hearts. They'll grow so keen
They'll wonder what they'd ever seen
In that ridiculous machine,
That nauseating, foul, unclean,
Repulsive television screen!
And later, each and every kid
Will love you more for what you did.

FUNNY POEMS

…………………

That's not my age; it's just not true.
My heart is young; the time just flew.
I'm staring at this strange old face,
And someone else is in my place!

My body's not in disrepair.
I've not much grey in my brown hair.
I sometimes feel a little tired
But go for jogs when I'm inspired.

This old age thing is not for me.
Concessions given, prescriptions free.
I'll just pretend I'm in my prime.
To age too fast would be a crime.

I'm just not 60 in my head.
It's still so long till I am dead,
So please don't see me in that way.
I'm staying young, if that's OK!

……………………

The people upstairs all practise ballet
Their living room is a bowling alley

Their bedroom is full of conducted tours.
Their radio is louder than yours,
They celebrate week-ends all the week.
When they take a shower, your ceilings leak.
They try to get their parties to mix
By supplying their guests with Pogo sticks,
And when their fun at last abates,
They go to the bathroom on roller skates.
I might love the people upstairs more
If only they lived on another floor.

……………………..

The grass needs cutting,
I must mend the gate.
I'm expecting a parcel,
I hope it's not late.
I must get a wash on.
There's the ironing too.
The gas bill needs paying.
There's so much to do.
I must send that email.
I can't really moan,
This is the life,
When you're working from home.

I'm due a long lie in
I must feed the cat.

FUNNY POEMS

There's the dishes to do,
I'll get round to that.
I'll de-frost the freezer
If I've got time,
But I'm watching the cricket.
Sky Sports is just fine!
I'll look at that spreadsheet,
Use my mobile phone,
So everyone knows
That I'm working from home.

....

You find you're getting hairier though not atop your head.
You somehow sustain injuries while sleeping in your bed.
Your arm is not quite long enough to make the fine print clear.
You walk into a room then think - Now why'd I come in here?

You only use your mobile phone to send texts and to talk.
You don't change into workout gear just to take a walk.
You phone in for your takeout and you pick up your own order.
You need your kids to help set up the new HD

recorder.

You frequent ATMs so you can have some cash on hand.
You venture to the beach but just to walk along the sand.
Before going somewhere new, you check the parking situation.
Your generation's music now plays on the oldies station.

You type a text one handed using just your index finger.
You'd struggle to identify a top ten song or singer.
When faced with going out at night you'd rather watch TV.
Sitting cross-legged on the floor is a distant memory.

You don't trust direct debit and you still get paper bills.
It's starting to get harder to keep track of all your pills.
You keep forgetting passwords, so you now just have the one.
You're alarmed to find your surgeon looks ridiculously young.

Most things are sagging lower but your waistband's sitting higher.
When scrolling to your year of birth your finger starts

to tire.
You no longer feel confident when climbing up a ladder.
A good chunk of your nighttime is spent emptying your bladder.

You miss the end of movies 'cause you can't help nodding off.
You're not sure which is harder, bending down or straightening up.
TV shows are hard to follow because all the actors mumble.
Your friends no longer laugh when you trip or take a tumble.

Instead of squeezing pimples you're now plucking out stray hairs.
Loud music now annoys you but your television blares.
You find yourself declaring things like, "It will outlast me!"
Your doctor recommends you get a colonoscopy.

Regardless of how many of these signs apply to you,
A healthy sense of humour is the key to help you through.
Laughter's the best medicine, life needn't be so bleak.

FUNNY POEMS

Just don't laugh too hard in case you spring a little leak!

…………………………

I need to lose weight, just a pound or twenty.
If I could lose fifty, well that would be plenty.
I could join a gym, but I don't have the gumption.
My legging clad legs aren't for public consumption.

My exercise bike is succumbing to rust
And only gets touched when I really must dust.
And much like a pet in need of attention,
It made me feel guilty (and slack not to mention).

The solution, of course, was such a no brainer.
I bought it a mate...an elliptical trainer!
This is quite easy! Or so I reckoned
When I tried it in store for a whole fifteen seconds.

But once it was home and I tried it for longer,
The pain in my side was all that got stronger.
I puffed and I gasped, till I couldn't breathe.
Kicked off at nine, it was now nine oh three.

Of course! The resistance must be way too high
But no, it read zero; I thought I might cry.
The six on the dial sat silently mocking,

FUNNY POEMS

My level of fitness was really quite shocking.

Motivation was all that I saw myself losing,
And my self-esteem was taking a bruising.
I tried it to music but all that achieved
It drowned out the sound of my poor creaking knees.

This instrument of torture could go take a hike.
I glanced now with longing at my trusty bike.
I couldn't recall why we had parted ways.
Climbed up on the seat and thought, Happy days!

I pedalled with gusto, but soon I remembered...
It felt like my buttocks were being dismembered.
The padding on my derrière is quite thick,
So why does it feel like I'm perched on a brick?

It was just all too hard; I gave up in disgust.
My plan to lose weight was clearly a bust.
Oh well...at least I can say that I tried it.
I mean, really, I can't be expected to diet!

....

CPSIA information can be obtained
at www.ICGtesting.com
Printed in the USA
LVHW010952281122
734044LV00009BA/342

9 789356 754218